Eric Stanway

The Old Rindge House

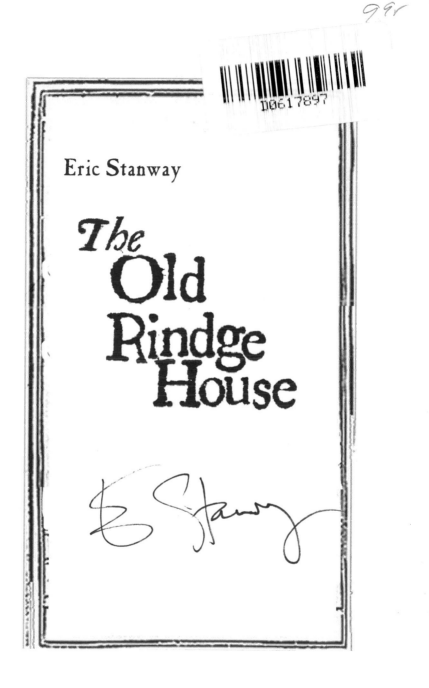

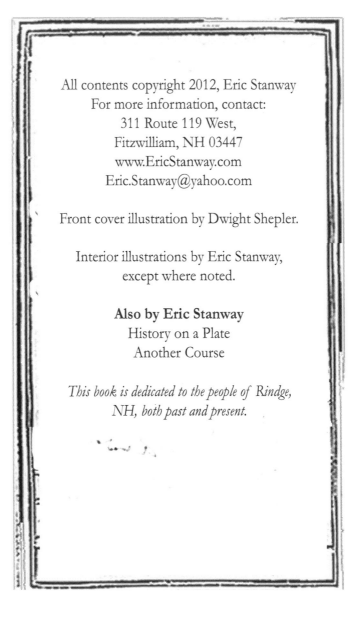

Front cover illustration by Dwight Shepler.

Interior illustrations by Eric Stanway,
except where noted.

Also by Eric Stanway
History on a Plate
Another Course

*This book is dedicated to the people of Rindge,
NH, both past and present.*

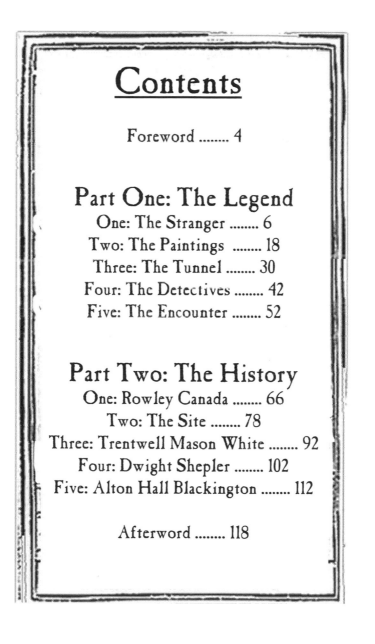

Contents

Foreword

A book such as this one cannot possibly be written in a vacuum; many people have come forward during its creation.

First and foremost is Robert Cleland of the Rindge Historical Society, who has been indispensible as he provided guidance and significant amounts of information on the history of the area. Amy Raymond, of the same society, scoured the area in an attempt to locate the site of the Old Rindge House. Alan Couture, a resident on Abel Road, gave me significant insight into the site itself. Lesley University, Yankee Magazine and The Boston Herald graciously allowed me to use the source material found in this volume. Additionally, Katharine Schillemat, Administrative Assistant of the Historical Society of Cheshire County, provided me with a wealth of information about the Peirce family.

Last but not least, I must thank the owners of the property that now sits on the site of the Old Rindge House, for allowing me to take photographs there.

Eric Stanway
December 15, 2011

Part One:
The Legend

One: The Stranger

The farmer stared grimly down at the village, which lay below, shrouded by cold fog. The year of our Lord 1817 had proven to be catastrophic. His eyes ran over the houses bordering on the frozen pond below. Here, in West Rindge, New Hampshire, famine was looking like a real possibility.

The farmer had been working the land on the old Peirce homestead his whole life, and seen his share of troubles. Now, however, things were reaching the breaking point.

This was an unforgiving place at the best of times; the ground was hard and rocky, and each spring thaw brought new chunks of granite to the surface, big enough to break a plow. The winters were long and cold, and it could be many months between deliveries of supplies, as they had to be carried over make-shift and muddy roads.

The people here were as hard as their environment; a quiet, steadfast breed, economical with their words, no-nonsense in their approach. Privation was a regular companion, and it shaped their character. But recent events had pushed even this hardy breed to the brink of desperation.

The previous year had been with-out any summer whatsoever. The crops had withered and died, bring-ing famine to the town. A dry fog had reddened the atmosphere, turn-ing the very air to a hue of dark ochre. Some people said it was a sign from the heavens, and that all of their past sins were coming due.

As each day and month progressed, the sun remained little more than a pale white disk. And every time one turned around, it seemed, the price of basic supplies increased by leaps and bounds. Snow had fallen in June of last year, and the cost of oats had risen from 12 cents to 92 cents a bushel. People were being forced from their homes, and had to seek what living they could scrape up on the open road.

In this village, an air of tangible depression had set in, and many were beginning to question if the world itself were coming to an end. The new bell that had been hung in the village church the past February was meant to spread the word of the Almighty among the flock; instead of instilling hope among the residents, however, it sounded more like a harbinger of doom.

These dark musings plagued the farmer's mind as he nailed boards onto the wall of his barn, in a futile attempt to stop it from disintegrating. The cold wind whistled over the bare ridge, and he could see his knuckles turning blue. Shivering, he stumbled down from his ladder and stared for a moment into the dark horizon. Clouds were settling over the peak of Mount Monadnock, gunmetal gray and threatening. Below, in the village, the dry fog had settled over the water, blocking out the houses on the far side of the pond. The skeletal branches of the trees on the horizon clawed at the ominous sky.

It was turning out to be another difficult winter, he thought bitterly, and it didn't look like any shipments were coming in before spring. Everybody was hungry, and the roads were already blocked by snow.

Walking to the edge of the ridge, he turned about and inspected the house. It was a plain, square structure, devoid of exterior ornaments. It had been built many years ago, of the basic New England design. Two stories high, it held three rooms on each floor, and several more in the ell that stretched out on the eastern side. The paint had long since peeled from the wood, and it lay bare and gray, open to the elements. A few struggling apple trees hung onto their rocky perch behind the house, around which several sheep fought for whatever they could find under the freshly-fallen snow.

Reluctantly, the farmer had

reached the conclusion that the place was just too large for him to manage by himself. The clapboards were coming loose on the front; he would have to deal with that tomorrow. There were leaks in the roof, as well. If this winter was anything like the last one, they would be in real trouble before the spring.

A terrible scream ripped the air, echoing through woods behind the house. Bobcats, he mused. They're hungry, too. He scanned the forest, and his eyes settled on the small cemetery at the bottom of the yard. He realized that his family was sleeping there, and he might well be joining them soon.

"Husband, are you finished?" His wife was coming around the side the house, holding her arms and shivering. She had been the prettiest girl in town when he married her; but the years of living up on this hill had taken their toll. Deep lines coursed her face and those lips he had once coveted were pursed with strain.

"Almost, wife," he said absently. "The wind is getting too much for me. I'll start early in the morning."

"Very well," she said, turning away. Then, over her shoulder: "Dinner's ready."

The farmer went back to the barn and began collecting his tools. A light snow had begun to fall, and he looked up at the menacing sky. The clouds were rolling like a pot of soup over a high fire. He shook his head. He could smell a storm coming. Again.

ભ   ભ   ભ

The farmer settled himself

down at the table as his wife ladled him a bowl of oatmeal from the pot on the fire. He still couldn't feel his hands, and tucked them under his armpits to try and force some warmth into them.

"Did you finish fixing the barn wall?" she asked as she sat down with her own bowl.

"No, I didn't finish fixing the barn wall," he said, and could hear the petulance in his own voice. He clumsily grabbed his wooden spoon and shoved oatmeal into his mouth. "I'll do it first thing in the morning," he added.

"Um," she muttered, and ate. The wind was picking up, and the windows rattled in response.

"It looks like a bad one," he observed. "We might not see a shipment of grain for some time."

"We're no worse off than anyone else in the village," she said.

They ate in silence. The wind picked up outside the house, and pulled at the walls.

Then, a hammering at the door.

They both sat up, staring at it.

The hammering began again.

"Stay here," the farmer whispered. "I'll get it."

He got up and walked over to where his gun stood, leaning against the wall. He trod silently to door, and then called:

"Who is it?"

"For God's sake, let me in!" came the reply.

The farmer unlatched the door, and opened it slightly. Without, stood the shivering figure of a man. He held a small black box under his left arm. Icicles hung from his beard and the brim of his hat.

"What do you want?" the farmer demanded, his rifle at the ready.

"Shelter," the man managed through chattering teeth. "I'm more than willing to work for room and board."

"Let him in," his wife called. "It's not fit for man nor beast out there."

The farmer waved him through with his gun, still wary. Ice and snow fell from the man's coat as he walked slowly into the room. He pulled off his hat, to reveal a patch of wild hair. His face was young and unlined, but his eyes held a deep sadness.

"What's your name?" the farmer asked.

"John Smith," the man replied. "I've come a long way, and I need work."

The farmer allowed himself a

smile. "I need a worker," he said. "If you're willing to put your shoulder into it, you're welcome here."

"Come on, sit down," the wife called. "You're welcome to a bowl of this porridge."

"Thank ye, ma'am," the man said. He put his box down on the floor and then hurried over to the fireplace, and began chafing his hands over the flames. A bowl of porridge was offered, and he sat down to eat.

"You can sleep in the front room," the wife said. "I'll get you some blankets."

"You're very kind.," Smith said.

"Where are you from?" the farmer asked.

Smith paused, and looked down at his bowl. He was quiet for a while.

"I've come a long way," he said at last. "I'm willing to work."

Two: The Paintings

The farmer arose before dawn the next morning, not quite ready to face another day of hard work. Groaning, he climbed out of bed and pulled on his shirt. Upon entering the parlor, he was surprised to discover that his wife was already up, and poking at a blazing fire in the hearth.

"Where's Mr. Smith?" he asked, looking around.

"He's gone to draw water from the well," his wife replied. "He's already brought in wood and stacked it, and lit the fire."

At that moment, the man walked in, carrying two large buckets. "Good morning," he said.

"And to you. An early start," said

the farmer. "I like that. We'll milk the cows, and have breakfast. Then we'll get to fixing the barn."

"Sounds good to me," Smith said. "I'm not afraid to work. I can handle an axe and a hammer, and what I don't know, I'm willing to learn."

The farmer's wife boiled water, poured some oats into the pot. "You said you've come a long way," she said. "Where are you from?"

"I wouldn't like to say," Smith said. "I'm trying to forget the past."

"A bad love affair?" the farmer ventured.

"You might say that," the man replied. "It's better buried and done."

There was an uncomfortable silence in the room.

"Fine by me," the farmer said. "As long as your back is strong and your arms are sure, that's all I ask."

☙   ☙   ☙

Though the day was short, the work moved quickly. With two people at the job, the side of the barn was fixed well before the end of the day, and secured against the wind. Throughout it all, Smith said hardly a word, preferring the sound of the axe and the hammer to his own voice. And, though the wind whipped mercilessly through their clothes, the man uttered not one complaint. Doggedly, he kept on toiling.

That evening, as they sat down to dinner, Smith spoke for the first time in hours.

"You noticed that box I brought with me?" he asked.

"I saw it, but I didn't want to

inquire," the farmer's wife replied. "What's in it?"

"I'll show you," Smith said, and got up to walk into the front room.

The farmer and his wife shot each other an uneasy look, and then turned to Smith as he came back. He put the box down on the table and opened it.

Lifting the lid, he pulled a number of small bags and vials, along with brushes, and laid them reverently on the table.

"I'm an artist," he said. "Well, I used to be." He turned to the farmer. "I want to offer you a proposition. I've noticed that the front room is just bare plaster. At night, when the work is done, I'd like to paint murals on that room - farming scenes, vases of flowers, things like that."

"That sounds very nice," said

the wife. "Many rich folk have such things in their houses - I've seen them myself."

"Well, I suppose it's all right with me," the farmer said. "So long as it doesn't interfere with the work."

"It won't," the man replied. "I have my pigments here. I'll grind them up in the cellar and mix them, so it won't mess up the house."

"That's all right, then," the farmer said, and the matter was settled.

આ   આ   આ

As time went on at the farm, things settled into a routine. During the day, Smith and the farmer would work on the house, battening down boards and fixing leaks. At night, after supper, Smith would retire to his room, as the farmer smoked his pipe and gazed into the fire, and his wife sewed or read the Bible.

As the evening wore on, they could hear him puttering around the room, as a sliver of light came from under the door. Even after they retired for the night, the man worked on, mixing his paints and working on the murals.

Every morning, Smith was the first man up, stacking the wood, getting the water, and putting on the fire. One morning, at breakfast, the farmer's wife asked how the murals were coming along.

"I'm getting there," Smith said.

"I'd like to see the paintings, if it's all right with you," the farmer ventured.

"Well, I don't like to show my artwork before it's finished. I'd rather you waited on it."

"An artist's temperament," said the wife. "Very well, Mr. Smith. We'll wait until you're done."

A terrible storm blew in over the next few days, and the roads were rendered impassible by the snow. Huge drifts blanketed the hills, sheathing the landscape in a glistening blanket of white. Traffic on the roads came to a complete standstill. A cold killing fog wrapped itself around the base of the trees, sought out nooks and burrows where small animals slept. Silence reigned, except for the muffled creaking of branches weighed down with ice.

At the old Peirce homestead, the farmer was smoking his pipe as he hunched close to his fire, trying to glean as much warmth as he could from the meager flames. Without, sleet was rattling against the windows and the wind was howling away. His wife came over with three bricks, which she placed by the side of the fire to warm, so they could be put into the beds.

"It's a filthy night out there," she observed at last.

"Um," the farmer grunted, and blew out a mouthful of pipe smoke.

She motioned toward the front room. "Perhaps Mr. Smith would like a cup of tea, to warm his bones."

"You could ask him," the farmer replied, not taking his eyes from the fire.

She went to the door, and knocked. "Mr. Smith? I was wondering if you'd like a cup of tea."

No response. She turned briefly to her husband, and then knocked again.

"Mr. Smith?"

Still nothing. She turned to her husband. He looked up, annoyed.

"He must be there," he said. "He can't have gone anywhere."

She knocked louder. "Mr. Smith? Are you all right?"

The farmer got up and walked toward the door. "John," he called. "Is anything amiss?"

Still, there was no response from the room. The farmer looked briefly at his wife, and then turned his attention to the door. "I'm coming in," he announced, and turned the knob.

The door creaked piteously on its hinges as it swung slowly open. Within, the lights were still burning, and the couple saw the painted room for the first time. Green hills and fields stretched along the walls, topped by large white houses and cut across with fences. A shepherd lay lazily below a tree, idly playing his pipe, as his herd grazed contentedly in nearby meadows. On another wall, fishing huts dotted a rugged shoreline, and inlets stretched into shallow marshes. A man was desperately trying to pull his boat ashore, wading through reeds and cattails.

The farmer and his wife gazed at the tableau in astonishment and silence. The candles flickered and seemed to lend animation to the figures on the walls. An artist's pallet and paints lay on a nearby wooden table. The farmer dipped his finger into one of the smears, and discovered it was still wet.

Of the painter, however, there was no sign. The only sound was that of the wind and the sleet, pounding impatiently on the windowpanes.

"But ... where is he?" the wife

asked. Her voice sounded thin and empty in the room.

"He can't have disappeared into thin air," the farmer said, doubting himself even as he said the words. He began to examine the walls, as if the answer might be found there. Eventually, he came to the fireplace.

"Wife, bring a candle! Quickly!"

She did as she was bid. The farmer was running his fingers over the rough wood of the mantelpiece, and snatched the candle from her as she approached. Placing the flickering light over the wood, they managed to discern a crude inscription:

"J. Smith painted this room, 1817."

Without, the wind continued to scream.

Three: The Tunnel

T he next morning, the snow lay thick upon the hills, glistening like diamonds in the milky light. Though the storm had cleared, a cold, biting wind still whistled along the top of the ridge, and all was silent except for its howling causing the trees to wave and creak.

In the full light of day, the farmer and his wife made a thorough search of the area surrounding the house, but found no footprints to mark the departure of their guest. The man's disappearance had them both completely baffled. The shutters, which had proven a formidable defense against wandering bands of Mohawk and Otter Indians, were still securely in place, and the iron hinges holding them were locked. There was no way anyone could have escaped from the house. The mystery had them both perplexed.

ଔ   ଔ   ଔ

In desperation, the farmer sought help from some of his neighbors, a most of which agreed to help him find the man. It was a ragged, unkempt group that made up the search party, as they tromped from hill to hill, calling out for Smith, but to no avail. Eventually, fatigue took its toll, as vocal chords grew hoarse from yelling, and fingers and toes turned blue from cold.

It fell to Richard Kimball, a Methodist preacher, to disclose the facts to the farmer, at last.

"This is sheer folly," he declared

as the night began to fall. "The man is gone; that much is clear. If he were anywhere in the vicinity, he would have made himself known by now."

"I suppose you're right," the farmer admitted. "It just taxes my conscience to think of him, out alone, in this forbidding wilderness."

Kimball laid a reassuring hand on his shoulder. "Rest easy, my son," he said. "You have done everything a good Christian should. You offered shelter and sustenance to the way-ward soul; it's not your fault that he should have left."

"But there were no footprints," the farmer replied. "He left no sign of his departure. It's as if the earth itself had swallowed him up."

Kimball paused, gazed up at the frigid white sky. "It's not for us to question God's will," he pronounced.

"If the lost lamb chooses to remain lost, so be it."

With this, the men repaired to the farmhouse, where the farmer's wife had a hot pot of coffee waiting.

ᴄ෪   ᴄ෪   ᴄ෪

Several days passed without incident at the farm. The farmer soon felt the loss of his workmate, as he toiled to keep the elements at bay, fixing and repairing the crumbling structure.

One afternoon, as he hauled an armful of wood toward the house, he could feel his feet giving way beneath the crust of snow. Yelling, he dropped the wood, even as he slid into a morass of mud. He clawed at the ground, trying to gain purchase, as a black hole swallowed him up.

Pain shot through his back as he

hit the bottom of the pit. He lay there for a moment, trying to gather his senses. All around him, black rocks were piled up, and he could hear ice falling about him from the top of the hole. Rubbing his knees, he got slowly to his feet, and looked around.

It was a tunnel. On each side, he saw an impenetrable veil of darkness. Above, the white sky gazed down, apathetic to his plight.

"Wife!" he yelled. "Come quick!"

He continued to shout for some time, with no response. Eventually, her head appeared over the rim of the pit, looking down at him, her eyes full of concern.

"Are you injured?" she asked.

"I'm all right," he said, brushing himself off. "I'm in a tunnel. Bring me some light, would you?"

It was a while before she reappeared with a lamp. Gingerly, she handed it down to him, and he waved it about, to reveal wet rocks surrounding him on both sides.

Behind him, the tunnel stretched back to the fieldstone foundations of the house. In the other direction, nothing. He decided to explore, and ventured into the darkness.

The tunnel floor was slippery and wet, and he had to steady himself as he went along, holding onto the wall with one hand and trying desperately to keep the lamp upright with the other. There was no sound except for his footsteps and the ragged echo of his own breathing.

Eventually, the passage opened up, and he found himself in a small room. He flashed the light about, and, as he made out the contents, he recoiled in horror.

Coffins were tumbled about in the recess, many of them broken open, spilling their contents onto the floor. The floor was littered with bones, broken and yellowed with age. The empty eye sockets of skulls glared at him mockingly.

He flashed the light on the coffin plates. He could make out some of them, and recognized the names of several of his ancestors. Others were probably neighbors from the village.

The stench of mold and decay was everywhere, and he gagged with revulsion as he backed out into the tunnel. He realized he was directly underneath the cemetery at the bottom of his yard. Carefully, he made his way back through the tunnel, seeking sunlight.

Exploring under the foundation of his house, he found himself at the foot of a set of stairs, leading upward into the house itself. Carefully, he ascended the slimy steps, and found a firm oaken door barring his way. He came down the steps, and walked toward the opening in the tunnel ceiling, and called for his wife again.

"Did you find anything?" she asked.

"Give me a hand here, woman," he said impatiently as he handed her the lamp and scrambled up out of the pit. She held his hand and lifted him up as he clawed at the rocks, and then lay there for a moment, his breath coming in clouds.

"It goes to the cemetery," he told her; "the other end is under the house."

"A tunnel? Under our house? Where does it come out?"

"I don't know. There was a door blocking my way. We'd better go and see."

They made their way back to the house, and warmed themselves a moment by the fire. The farmer walked to the window, and looked out into the back yard.

"I think it comes up in the front room," he concluded. "I'll go see."

Walking into Smith's room, he started pacing the walls, tapping occasionally with his fist. He looked out the window again, surveying the outer wall.

"It's definitely under this floor," he told her.

The wife began to follow her husband's lead, tapping at the walls and examining the floor. Eventually, she made her way to the mantelpiece, inscribed with the late tenant's signature.

"Husband! Come and look!" She was pulling on a small piece of diamond-shaped decoration on the mantel. "It's off center! That one, as well!"

The farmer came over and examined the woodwork. "You're right," he said. "They've been knocked loose." He turned it slightly, and a dull grating sound emanated from the left of the fireplace.

"What was that?" the wife asked.

"Try turning yours," the farmer said. She did so, and a panel to the left of the fireplace began to slide backward. Beyond, lay a black abyss.

She walked over to the table, picked up the candle, and waved it at the interior. The steps gleamed back at her, covered with moss and water.

The wife turned the ornament

back, and the board slid back into place. "Your grandfather must have put that there," she said. "In case of Indian attacks."

The farmer nodded his head in affirmation, and they headed out of the room, extinguishing the lights as they went.

"It still doesn't explain why Smith left so hurriedly," the farmer said as they walked into the parlor.

"We might never know; and we have important things to think about," his wife said as she went to the fireplace and extracted a key from a box on the mantel. She went over to the door of the front room, and locked it.

"I don't think we'll be needing the room for a while," she said.

Four: The Detectives

Life at the farm continued as usual for the next two weeks or so. The farmer and his wife had little time to dwell on the mystery of the artist as they went about their work, cleaning and fixing holes in the old house. The farmer put the whole incident in the back of his mind as he concentrated on repairing the roof, which was badly in need of his attention.

The wind whistled about his head as he pounded nails into the soffit, his hands cracked and bleeding from the cold. There was a nasty front coming from the west, and he was sure to lose a few of the shingles if this wasn't seen to.

"Halloa, there!"

The cry split the cold winter silence. The farmer strained around at the source, and saw two men heading up the road toward him. They were both bundled up in city clothes and looked well-fed. Even from this distance, he could tell they weren't from around here.

Wearily, the farmer descended the ladder, and went up to meet the men, as they were just reaching the top of the ridge. One was a burly fellow, probably in his thirties, with a red moustache. The other, thinner than his companion and of a pale complexion, hung back in deference.

"Stephen Benedict, of the Bayside Detective Agency," the heavy man said, extending a hand. "This is my associate, Mr. Richard Clark. Who do we have the honor of addressing?"

"My name's Peirce," the farmer replied as he shook his hand. "What can I do for you gentlemen?"

Benedict looked briefly at his companion, then back at the farmer. "It's about a missing man," he said. "A fellow by the name of Smith. You wouldn't know of him, would you?

"That depends," the farmer cagily said. "Is he in any kind of trouble?"

"Well, he certainly thinks he is. But, rest assured, our mission is benevolent. Do you know where he is?"

"It's too cold to stand out here, talking," said the farmer. "Come on in and have some coffee."

"Don't mind if we do, thank'ee," said Benedict. "We're pretty much frozen to the bone."

They went into the house, where

the farmer's wife was sweeping the floor. She looked up, wondering, as they entered the room.

"These are detectives, from Boston," the farmer explained. "They're looking for Mr. Smith."

"Mr. Smith? Why, has he done something?"

"We'd just like to talk to him," said Clark. "We have important news."

"Please, sit down," she offered. "I'll make some coffee."

"John Smith worked here on the farm for a spell," said the farmer. "Then, he disappeared, about two weeks ago. We haven't seen him since."

"Mr. Smith believes himself to be in a great deal of trouble," Benedict said. "His friends are concerned for his safety, and sent us out to find him."

"Well, we did organize a search party, but there's no sign of him anywhere around here," the farmer said. "He just vanished into the air."

"I'll be perfectly frank with you," Benedict announced, laying his hands on the table. "While in Boston, Mr. Smith developed a significant reputation as an artist. He had a wide range of admirers, including, apparently, one particular young woman.

"Unfortunately, one of his close friends had romantic designs on the same lady. Now, Smith could be the most amenable of men in most circumstances, but when demon drink took hold, he could become, shall we say, unmanageable."

"I've seen many a man become a beast when in his cups," said the farmer. "Sometimes, there is violence."

"And so it was in this case,"

Benedict agreed. "Jealousy between the two men escalated into murderous intent one night, when they were both drunk. A fracas ensued, the two of them fighting, throwing objects at each other, locked in mortal combat. As they struggled, the other man hit his head on the andiron in the fireplace, splitting his head."

"My goodness," the wife said as she poured the coffee. "I wouldn't have believed Mr. Smith to be capable of such behavior. Did the man die?"

"No, he's not dead," rejoined Clark. "His head was very badly injured, but it was mostly just blood. We have to surmise that, when Smith realized what had transpired, he panicked, and fled."

"Not only is the fellow not dead, but he feels badly about the entire episode," said Benedict. "When he realized that Smith was nowhere to be found, he put out word over the entire city, to try and find him. When that failed, he took out advertisements in the major newspapers, to the effect of all was forgiven, and he should return. That was also in vain; the notices went unanswered."

"He then turned to us," said Clark. "Through various sources, we discovered that he had traveled to New Hampshire. Further inquiries led us to this village, and your house."

"And that's where the trail ends," the farmer commented.

"It would appear so," said Clark.

The farmer rose from the table, went over to the fireplace, and pulled a small box from the mantel. Opening the lid, he extracted a key.

"Follow me," he said, and walked to the front room.

The two men rose from the table and did so, the wife walking behind.

"This was Smith's room," the farmer explained as he turned the lock.

"Excuse me," the wife said as she stepped between the men with a lamp. She walked into the room, and held it high, to show the panels.

The two detectives walked past the farmer, and followed her into the room, gazing in astonishment.

In the flickering light, the images seemed to take on a life of their own. The shepherd was still there, playing to his flock. The sheep seemed to ripple and shimmer as they plucked at the bright green grass. Behind, large white homes bestrode the tops of the hills, masters of their domain. On the far side, the fisherman was trying to get his boat ashore, his knees forever locked in the shallows. The large mill that stood behind had its wheel churning again, and water flowed copiously from the sluice. Three identical poplar trees held vigil on the hill behind.

The wife held the light closer to the wall, examining it more attentively than she had before.

"What's that, between the mill and the trees?" she wondered.

The three men followed her, and gazed into the background. The object stood there alone in the field, an orphan to its kind.

As they recognized the ominous silhouette, all of the people in the room sucked in a quick breath of air.

"It's a gravestone," the farmer said at last.

Five: The Encounter

And, really, that was that. The farmer was wrapped in thought as he watched the detectives take their leave. As they turned and waved to him, and he hailed back, he thought: well, that's the end of it, then.

A curious incident; something of a mystery; then it was back to the task of stopping the house from falling down. As he turned back to the house, he had the feeling that a chapter in his life had closed.

Life went back to its usual pattern as the year rolled on. For the first time in two years, spring spread across the land. That season melted into summer, the like of which the people of the town had not seen in

many a day. Famine became a dim
and distant memory for the people
of West Rindge, faced as they were
with all this bounty.

Fall came in, and with it the har-
vest. The people rejoiced in abun-
dance, piled baskets of apples and
pumpkins before the village church,
and thanked God for having taken
them into His fold once more.

The winter rolled in; the larders
and fruit cellars were full, and that
familiar feeling of desperation gave
way to optimism.

The farmer and his wife settled
down to an unaccustomed restful
winter. The roof was secure, the
walls battened down against the elements. The feed lots were full, and
there was little danger of losing any
of the animals. Thus it was that they
fell into their nightly ritual, the wife

doing her knitting, the farmer smoking his pipe and gazing into the fire.

"One year ago tonight," the wife commented out of nowhere. It was the first time she had spoken during most of the evening.

"What's that?" the farmer asked.

"Tonight. One year ago. That was when John Smith left us."

There was a long pause. The farmer smoked his pipe pensively. "I suppose you're right; I hadn't really thought of it. There's been no word of him since."

"It's one of those things," said the wife. "We might never know what happened."

There was suddenly a different pitch to the pounding of the sleet and snow against the windowpanes. A scratching, clawing sound seemed to echo through the room. The wind blew up from the valley, rattling the boards, shaking the structure. They both sat up, startled, as a furtive, rustling noise seemed to come from the outside of the house. They could hear footsteps, crunching through frozen snow, stumbling against the clapboards.

They stared at each other. The farmer made a motion with his hand, and they both remained quiet.

The footsteps came around again, this time at the back of the house. They weren't the sounds of an animal. Then, they stopped. The wind continued to howl.

The farmer silently got to his feet, walked over to the wall, where his gun stood. He examined it, and backed up against the side of the door.

His wife looked at him, her mouth imploring silently.

He opened the door. The storm blew in, throwing snow and ice across the floor. He headed out into the gale, staring around. His wife came up behind him and handed him a lantern. He waved it about the yard, seeing nothing but the rippling branches of the trees.

He headed off into the sleet. The night enveloped him as he walked into the back yard. His wife leaned out of the doorway, staring after him, as he disappeared.

She stood there for a few moments, clutching herself against the cold. The wind tore at her as she stared into the blackness, looking for movement.

Suddenly, a shrill scream ripped through the night.

The blood froze in the woman's veins. "Husband!" she called. "Are you there? Are you there?"

Panic gave her feet flight. She hurtled around the side of the house. As she made her way into the back yard, she could see the lantern, thrown into the snow. Beyond, lay the body of her husband, lying prone against a field of white.

She ran to him, clutched his head in her hands.

"Are you all right?" she implored, holding her face close to his.

He made some kind of inarticulate sound, and then threw his head back, his mouth open, his breath coming in thin, barely audible rattles, gradually fading to nothing. He lay back, his eyes open, staring blankly into the black sky.

She shouted his name, over and over, but he just lay there, still and rigid. Getting to her feet, she ran back to the house. She rushed to the stable, hitched the horse to the cart, and brought it into the front yard.

She then ran into back yard, where her husband still lay. Grabbing him under the armpits, she laboriously dragged him across the yard, where the horse stood, waiting.

Painfully, she managed to load her husband into the back of the cart, and climbing into the seat, urged the horse on into the thickening storm. As they headed down the hill, the trees on each side of the road whipped their branches menacingly. The ice and snow buffeted the carriage on both sides. But still, she whipped the horse on, the tears freezing on her cheeks as she tried to navigate her way to the doctor's house on the far side of town.

Finally, she reached his home,

climbed down, and ran to the front door, pounding on it and screaming.

"Let me in! Let me in! Let me in!"

At last, a light appeared in one of the windows. She could hear footsteps within, and then the door opened a crack, and a lined and sleepy face peered out at her.

"Who is it?"

"It's Mrs. Peirce, from down the road," she replied. "My husband! Something's happened to him!"

"I'll get my coat; wait there," the doctor said, and reappeared seconds later. The two of them walked over to the carriage, where the farmer still lay, his rigid form covered with snow and ice.

"Help me get him into the house," the doctor said. "I can't perform a diagnosis out here."

They grabbed him under both arms, and hauled him into the parlor. He uttered not a sound, gave no resistance, showed no sign of life.

They laid the man on the couch. He lay there, stiff and cold, his eyes staring vacantly. His mouth was formed into a rictus of terror, his jaw thrust out, protesting against an invisible menace.

The doctor pulled out his wooden trumpet, bared the man's chest, listened for few minutes; then he picked up his wrist, felt it, and laid it down.

He turned to the farmer's wife.

"I'm very sorry," he said. "Your husband is dead."

She fell into a paroxysm of despair, shrieking as she dropped to the floor. The doctor pulled her up by the shoulders, looked into her eyes.

"What happened?"

"There was a prowler," she sobbed. "He went out behind the house. There was a terrible cry. I went after him, and found him there … like this."

The doctor stood up, looked down at his patient.

"I'm afraid there's nothing we can do for him," he said. "But if, indeed, there was a prowler, we should try to find his footprints before they're obliterated by the snow."

Despite her grief, she saw sense in this, and agreed.

Bundling up, the two of them left the house, and walked into the yard, where the storm was still raging. The doctor helped her into the cart, and they drove the horse back up the road.

It was a silent journey. The doctor concentrated on keeping the rig on the road while the woman beside him sobbed quietly to herself. Eventually, they came to the ridge, and drove up the dirt road that led to the house.

The door was open, whipping fiercely about in the wind. The doctor shut it, and turned to the farmer's wife.

"Which way?" he asked.

Mutely, she pointed to the back yard. The doctor followed her lead, and walked into the yard, waving his lantern before him. The wife followed behind.

The doctor stopped, staring at the expanse of white before him. He could see the farmer's footprints, and those of his wife. But nothing else.

"But there was someone here!" the wife protested.

"I believe you," the doctor said. "But, whoever - or whatever - it was, left no trace whatsoever."

The two of them stood silently for a while, staring into the yard. Beyond, the cemetery stood silent, keeping its secrets to itself. The wind continued to bear down on the ridge, and the trees swayed and bucked in sympathy. Above, the snow fell, apathetic to the tragedy.

To this day, nobody has been able to say what became of the artist, or what visitation it was that drove the farmer to a terrified death.

Part Two:
The History

One: Rowley Canada

Dwight Shepler's Sept. 23, 1934 article, "The Ghostly Mystery of the Old Rindge House," which was published in The Boston Herald.

O ver the years, I have discovered that you really don't have to go far to find the strange and exotic. There's a popular presumption out there that maintains, in order to find adventure, you have to travel far afield. I find that people frequently ignore the wonders that can be found almost in their own back yards.

The germ of this particular adventure came one afternoon as I was browsing in a knick-knack store in the middle of Troy, New Hampshire. The place was full of the usual items one might expect to find - old kitchen implements, plates commemorating long-lost anniversaries, gadgets that people might have used once and then consigned to the reject pile.

But there, between the 50-cent VHS tapes and old vinyl records, was something very special.

It was a clipping from The Boston Herald, dated Sunday, September 23, 1934. The article must have captured the attention of an editor at the time, as it was accorded a full page, replete with illustrations. The title of the piece was "The Ghostly Mystery of the Old Rindge House," by Dwight Shepler. It basically recounted the tale I have presented in the first half of this book, with some added notations. The whole clipping had been lovingly pasted to a large piece of cardboard at some point, and time had weathered it to a brittle yellow, the hue of dry autumn leaves.

The tale captivated me at once, and, smelling a story, I purchased it on the spot.

Now, I live in Fitzwilliam, and Troy is the next town over. Rindge sits to the east of these towns, along what is now Route 119. It's a fairly large town, and is comprised of three villages; East Rindge, Rindge Center and West Rindge.

It is this last village with which we are primarily concerned. West Rindge dates back to 1730, when it received a grant from the Commonwealth of Massachusetts. In those days, the town was known as Rowley Canada, and was settled by soldiers and descendants of soldiers who fought in Canada during

King William's War (1690-1697).

A word or two on this conflict is in order, as it illustrates how foreign affairs affected the colonies at the time. King James II (1633-1701) came to the British throne on February 6, 1685. Unlike his predecessor, Charles II, he was an extremely religious man, of a distinctly Popish persuasion, and began to actively attempt to convert the largely Protestant citizens of England.

This did not go over well. James was forced to flee to France in 1688, where he found sympathy in the French king, Louis XIV. In his absence, his daughter, Mary, and her husband, William of Orange, became joint sovereigns.

Louis would have none of this. He denounced the new monarchy in the strongest possible terms, and declared that the people of the nation should not have the right to switch rulers.

Things started to become heated in America, as King William rejected an offer of colonial neutrality. Long-standing conflicts involving the fisheries and fur trades escalated into full-blown war.

The first blow in the battle was struck in Dover, New Hampshire, at the instigation of Louis de Buade, Comte de Frontenac et de Palluau (1622 -1698), governor of Canada. A group of Indian women showed up at the home the aged Major Richard Waldron one night in July, 1689. They asked for lodging, and were admitted to the house. Later that night, they

A contemporary woodcut entitled "Night Attack of Indians on Major Waldron's House, Dover, NH" depicts an event in the Cochecho Massacre, the attack of June 28, 1689 on Dover, New Hampshire. Major Richard Waldron was brutally tortured by the Indians during the attack and slain with his own sword.

arose, and let in a large group of their tribesmen, who were waiting in ambush. Waldron was tortured to death, and the town burned to the ground. In the fracas, 23 of the townspeople were killed outright, and 29 others captured. The town of Penaquid, Maine, met a similar fate a month later. These events galvanized the British colonists to action.

The resulting war pretty much decimated the coffers of Connecticut, New York and Massachusetts. The latter was particularly hard-hit, and letters of credit were issued to the tune of 40,000 pounds. Sir William Phipps of Maine was sent to England to seek help from the king, but he had his own problems, and determined that the colonies should

MONADNOCK MOUNTAIN & LAKE
View from the North. From a Drawing by C.K.Mason, Dublin.   Elevation above the Sea. 3,450 feet

Image courtesy The Jaffrey Historic District Commission
Monadnock Mountain & Lake. View from the North.
From a Drawing by C.W. Mason, Dublin. Elevation above
the Sea, 3,450 feet. From the Map of Cheshire County,
1858.

fight their own battles. The war pretty much dragged on for a few more years, until a peace treaty was signed in 1697.

It fell to the veterans and descendants of this war to settle the new town of Rowley Canada, an area comprised primarily of wetlands and rocky outcroppings. According to the History of Cheshire and Sullivan Counties (1886), an allowance was made for 10,000 acres, including ten large ponds and "a large shrub swamp," which has since been ceded to the Town of Sharon.

This swamp was known as a "Tophet Swamp," and held sinister associations for the colonists. It is a term peculiar to the residents of the Massachusetts Bay Colony, and literally means "place of burning."

A 19th-century engraving depicting the sacrifice of children to the god Moloch at Tophet, a place in the Valley of Hinnon, outside Jerusalem. As colonists in New England overheard the rituals of native peoples in the swamps, they were reminded of this story, and attributed the name "Tophet" to the wetlands in the area.

The word refers to a place in the Valley of Hinnon, near Jerusalem, used for idolatrous worship and the sacrifice of children. The root of the word comes from the Hebrew "toph," which means "drum." It is thought that drums were being beaten to drown out the cries of children, who were burned to death in the rites of the god Moloch.

As native people were inclined to hold Shamanistic rituals in these areas, the bonfires and sounds of drums must have scared the living daylights out of the former Europeans. For these pious people, hell was never really very far from their minds.

Two: The Site

Photograph by the author

The site of the Old Rindge House, as it stands today. If you compare this photo with Shepler's illustration at the beginning of this section, you can see the distinctive hump at the right hand side of the ridge, and can just make out the old road in the center, which leads to the site.

A bel Road runs along the perimeter of Pearly Pond, a large body of water with numerous waterways and wetlands. Over the years, various mills were built along this area, which once supported a thriving woodworking industry. You can still see the foundations of one of the mills, right by the side of the road.

Following along the road, you come upon the wetlands, home of the abandoned village mentioned in the legend. Further up is the ridge itself, once home to the Old Rindge House. There has been a lot of building in this area as of late, and numerous large houses stand on what was once pasture.

Writer Dwight Shepler described the area as it stood in 1934 in his Boston Herald article:

"Standing lone and dark on a barren drumlin hill, the structure is the forbidding guardian of the secrets of the life that went on in the deserted village that once stood in the valley below it.

"Years of snow, sleet and rain have eaten deep into the grain of its clapboards. Gales have torn away its shingles and its ridge-pole, and its tenant of a short year has reconstructed the upper story with tarpaper. The ell has fallen into decay and has been removed, and a yawning cellar hole marks its boundaries. Thieves have stolen mantelpieces, newel posts and other pieces of interior architectural detail. But the strange

Photograph by the author
The disused road leading up to the Old Rindge House,
now largely overgrown. Most of the trees in this photograph are only about 40 to 50 years old.

paintings have stayed on the firm plaster of the walls, and, though faded and mellowed by the decades, they are still visible in full detail.

"This house is the last really articulate remnant of a community which flourished in the New Hampshire hills before the memory of the oldest resident. Lost in the trees and thickets of the little valley below, the indistinct remains of the foundations of a dozen houses can be found when you know that they are there. These dwellings of forgotten souls faced on a street, at the end of which stood a mill on the edge of a stream. The wheels of the machinery are skeletons of rust, almost completely disintegrated by erosion."

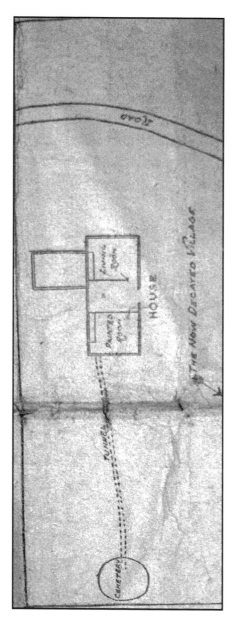

Image courtesy The Boston Herald Dwight Shepler's 1934 map of the Old Rindge House. Abel Road stands to the right hand side of the image.

Finding this spot, even given the relatively brief period since the house's destruction, was no easy task. I spent several days combing through the woods along the road, coming up with little other than an ancient cow scapula and the attention of the local police, who were alerted by local residents.

Discouraged after about three days of such foraging, I decided to take a new tack. I walked the length of Abel Road, until I was suddenly struck by a shallow wetland to my left, and a ridge standing at the top of it. A long-abandoned road led to the top of the hill, and I could picture Shepler's illustration from the Boston Herald.

Standing at the bottom of the ridge, you can clearly see where the house once stood, and the

Photograph by the author
The cemetery that still stands behind the the site of the Old Rindge House. This spot marks the last resting place of Benjamin Peirce, Josiah Peirce and his wife Azubah.

road leading up to it. Unfortunately, the site itself has fallen victim to development, as there is a house and a large driveway right at the site of the old cellar hole. Behind the house, however, the cemetery still stands, in an admittedly horrible state of disrepair. The obelisk that once marked the site is now on its side, and the other stones are missing. Local resident Eric Poor, who used to hunt deer on this site some 20 years ago, shed a little light on the old inscriptions, stating that it marks the last resting place of Benjamin Peirce, Josiah Peirce and his wife Azubah.

The present resident of the house that sits on the site says that obelisk fell over some years ago, and has never been righted.

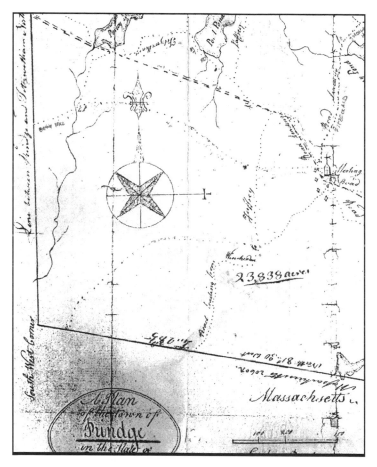

Image courtesy The Rindge Historical Society
A map of West Rindge, as drawn up in 1807. The dashed line in the center of the map indicates the present site of Route 119; the site of the Old Rindge House lies on the lower left hand side of the map, close to the Fitzwilliam border.

Further interviews with local residents revealed that there once was a proposal put forth by the Boy Scouts to repair the cemetery, which met with resistance by the then-owner of the property. As the site is now private property, I would discourage any would-be archeologists from trespassing here, without first getting permission.

Some searching through "The History of The Town of Rindge" by Ezra S. Stearns (1875) revealed the following information:

"Benjamin Peirce, resided, a farmer, upon the old homestead. He married Dec. 8, 1813, Lucinda Allen, daughter of Eliphaz Allen. She died June 25, 1820, and he married Sarah (Gale) Raymond, of Winchendon. She died Feb.

9, 1851, and he married, Feb. 3, 1852, Mary (Coffin) Perkins, born March 12, 1790, widow of John Perkins, of Rindge and daughter of Deacon George and Abigail (Raymond) Coffin, of Winchendon. He died Jan. 8, 1858; his wife died July 10, 1856.

"Josiah Peirce was born in Lunenburg, Mass., Oct. 28, 1761. He was a son of Jonathan and Sarah (Dodge) Peirce, and a grandson of Ephraim and Esther (Shedd) Gould, of Rindge, and a nephew of the wife of Deacon John Lovejoy. It was this Ephraim Peirce who married for his second wife Huldah (Martyn) Wetherbee, widow of Hezekiah Wetherbee. Josiah married Nov. 14, 1782, Azubah Heywood, or Howard, who was born in Acton, Mass. Feb.

Photo by the author

One of the old cellar holes that marks the deserted village that stands close to Pearly Pond in West Rindge. The people who lived in these houses were primarily involved in the woodworking and lumber trades.

18, 1784, and removed to Rindge
in 1784. He was a respected citi-
zen, and resided in the south-west
part of the town. She died May
30, 1827, and he married Dec.
16, 1827, Polly Rugg, daughter of
Thomas Rugg, Senior. He died
Oct. 10, 1834."

This is where the gap between
legend and history makes itself
apparent. According to the story,
our unnamed farmer perished of
fright in the winter of 1818, but
there are no corresponding dates
on the stone, or in the records
of the family. At the point of
this writing, this discrepancy still
stands.

Three: Trentwell Mason White

Photo courtesy Lesley University
A photograph of Trentwell Mason White, taken in 1957.
At this time, he was President of Lesley University.

There are three writers who have, throughout history, turned their attention to this odd legend: Trentwell Mason White, a publisher in Boston; Dwight Shepler, a writer for The Boston Herald; and Alton Hall Blackington, a well known historian and raconteur.

White is a particularly elusive fellow; Google searches turn up little about the man excepting that he was president of Lesley University from 1944 to 1959. Dwight Shepler gives the following account of White's involvement in the story:

"We are indebted for the original version of the legend to

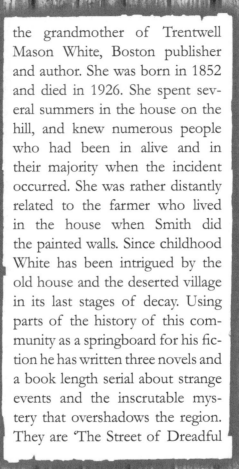

the grandmother of Trentwell Mason White, Boston publisher and author. She was born in 1852 and died in 1926. She spent several summers in the house on the hill, and knew numerous people who had been in alive and in their majority when the incident occurred. She was rather distantly related to the farmer who lived in the house when Smith did the painted walls. Since childhood White has been intrigued by the old house and the deserted village in its last stages of decay. Using parts of the history of this community as a springboard for his fiction he has written three novels and a book length serial about strange events and the inscrutable mystery that overshadows the region. They are 'The Street of Dreadful

Silence,' 'The Thing in The Road,' and 'Haunted Heights.'

"The other day, Mr. Bassett, who has lived in the house about a year, told me that 10 years ago, during a previous short tenancy, he had been plowing the stubborn soil of the hilltop when his horse fell up to his belly into a section of the tunnel which had not been filled in.

"The house had several passageways throughout the walls, and in the recently razed ell there was a secret room which Trentwell White had discovered a few years ago. For some time the house had been deserted, and White was prowling about it late one afternoon in an attempt to disclose more of its mysteries. He noticed for the first time that on the

second floor of the ell there was a space beneath the eaves that could not be logically filled by any room that appeared to the casual observer's eye. By trying all the pine panels of the wall of the adjacent room he found a door formed from three of the panels, and its rusted, invisible catches broke as he forced it open. Before him was a room, small and narrow, but finished enough to be livable, with dust more than an inch deep on the floor. Under the dust he found an old yellow piece of paper, the writing on it faded to invisibility.

"Darkness had fallen as White prepared to leave the house, and as he contemplated its history he began to hear sounds all around him. Things creaked on every hand,

and he thought he heard someone in the kitchen, in the back yard, and in the painted room. As he went down the stairs he fancied he heard a step behind him and sprayed his flashlight only to find nothing there. He had left the front door open, but now it was closed. He pushed it, but it failed to open. Then he applied his generous bulk to it with full force, driving his shoulder against the ancient wood. The door opened with a rush and White catapulted into the front yard, accompanied by the sound of a terrifying scream from the vicinity of the cemetery. Righting himself, he shot his flashlight toward the graveyard, but saw nothing. He didn't investigate, but he guesses it was a bobcat."

Bobcat or not, the house had

certainly developed an evil reputation by this point, and White's public talks on the subject only served to add fuel to the fire. Tales of hauntings prompted the curious to spend the night at the old house, to see for themselves what the spirits had to offer. Shepler's article in the Boston Herald spurred one such adventurer to offer his own brush with the supernatural in a letter to the editor dated Oct. 22, 1934:

"THAT HAUNTED HOUSE"

"To the Editor of the Herald:

'I was much interested in Dwight Shepler's account of the ghostly Old Rindge House. Four years ago, after listening to a talk given by Trentwell Mason White on the subject of this haunted house, two friends of mine and I went up to Rindge and spent the night in that famous painted room. We slept little and were constantly aware of mysterious noises throughout the house, none of which we investigated. While lying thus sleeplessly on an old mattressless bed, we had ample time to study what is perhaps the most mysterious bit of painting in the room, a weird circular design on the ceiling, which, for one brief, memorable moment, long after dark, became suddenly illuminated.

"I question the fact that the underground passage was dug by the artist, since most farmhouses of that period had such secret means of egress in case of Indian attacks. Besides, why should he dig his way out when there was nothing to prevent his going the customary way?

"Nevertheless, in my estimation, Mr. Bassett, the present tenant, is a very brave man.

"*HUBERT V. CORYELL, Jr., Lexington, Mass.*"

It would appear, from these accounts, that whatever spirits may have inhabited the house through its long and strange history, they were still quite active well into the 20th century, and were the subject of quite a deal of local lore.

Four: Dwight Shepler

Archives of American Art, Smithsonian Institution
Dwight Shepler drawing, ca. 1942, by an unidentified photographer.

We now come to the writer who started all of this off with his Boston Herald story. Dwight Shepler was born in Everett, Massachusetts and studied at the Boston Museum of Fine Arts, where he earned a BA degree in 1928. In the 1930s, he worked as an illustrator for the Boston Herald, Sun Valley and the Shell Oil Company.

During World War II, Shepler worked as a combat artist, painting many battle scenes from the Pacific theater, and won the Bronze Star. He also recorded action at the D-Day invasion in Normandy, and completed more than 300 combat scenes. Many of his illustrations appeared in Life magazine and American Heritage. He died in 1974.

Shepler seems to have been one of the last people to have seen the paintings in the Old Rindge House before its destruction, and the event appears to have left quite an impression. With the unflinching eye of an artist, he appraised John Smith's work at length:

"The paintings completely cover the walls of the first floor room to the left of the well-designed doorway. They are strange pastoral scenes, executed in oil, and rather crudely done from the standpoint of artistry. Although the general landscape and architecture is that of New England, discordant foreign elements tinge the design of the

Photo courtesy The Rindge Historical Society

This photo, taken in 1937, shows the ancient murals in the front room at the Old Rindge House. It is the only photograph of the paintings known to exist.

buildings; and the countryside of the Italian primitives, the Florentine school, and the Dutch school creeps into the execution of the hills and trees. The young man who painted them apparently had some knowledge of the methods of foreign painters, but the work suggests that these characteristics flowed from the brush of a man whose mind was on other things. The whole plan of the murals has no aim or order; incongruous elements absent-mindedly interject themselves into the design.

"The technique suggests that he was an unheralded harbinger of Picasso, Van Gogh, Cezanne, Matisse and the modern school. Distorted sheep and flat cows roam about, and proportions are bent and twisted to suit his fancy.

Image courtesy The Boston Herald

Dwight Shepler's drawing of the farmer's demise, from his Sept. 23, 1934 Boston Herald article, "The Ghostly Mystery of Old Rindge House."

"In one panel a shepherd blows his pipe beneath a spreading tree. He is clad in the garb of the turn of the 19th century, with a blue coat and long, tight-fitting white trousers. Beyond is a meadow with sheep before an Italian Renaissance hill, topped by houses and buildings that are American colonial with Byzantine influences. Another panel depicts a scene that suggests the fish houses of Rockport. Tidal inlets notch the shoreline, and a mill's undershot wheel pours forth water from an illogical source. The colonial houses look Moorish, while a man in the same garb of the 1800s leans precipitously as he pushes a rowboat from the back of a marsh.

"The third large wall space

represents a pasture scene, zig-zagged by white rail fences. A reclining cow of strange anatomy surveys a background of a New Hampshire meeting house and other smaller buildings. The church has a long ell of carriage stalls, many green-shuttered windows line its walls, while its steeple is an abortive Italian campanile painted white. Dutch trees dot the landscape.

"The skies are mellowed reds, greens and yellows. The ceiling has a central rosette in a bright color suggestive of Italy, while a similar decoration forms a band near the mantelpiece. Vases of flowers are painted in such a way as to give the impression that they were sitting on the now absent mantelpiece."

Actually, Shepler wasn't exactly the last one to see the paintings. In 1976, Clara Seymour of The Rindge Historical Society received a photograph and a letter from an old schoolmate, which said, in part:

"Recently, I came across a picture which you may recognize as one of the murals on the walls of the house on the Fitzwilliam Road, I think, where the overnight guest, a man who asked for shelter, decorated the walls and then disappeared.

"This is not a good picture, as the colors had faded even then, but the more you look at it, the more details you can discern.

"Hopefully, you have an artist friend or associate who could make or paint a copy in color. I thought I had at least two snaps of the other walls -- but, so far, they have not turned up."

The idea of there being more photographs out there is certainly an intriguing one; but, as of now, we will just have to be content with this one image of the long-lost paintings.

Five: Alton Hall Blackington

Photo from "More Yankee Yarns," by Solari
Alton Hall Blackington, broadcasting his show "Yankee Yarns" on WBZ Radio, Boston, in the 1940s.

For long-time New Englanders, Alton Hall Blackington needs little introduction. This beloved storyteller, known affectionately as "Blackie," was a fixture on WBZ radio in Boston for many years, recounting strange tales in his radio show, "Yankee Yarns." Born in 1893 in Rockland, Maine, he spent most of his life touring New England with a camera and a notebook, interviewing locals and dredging up strange and ancient legends.

For many years, Blackington worked on the staff of The Boston Herald, and wrote for numerous other publications, including Reader's Digest and Yankee magazine.

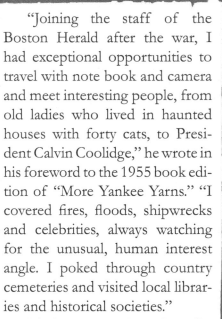

"Joining the staff of the Boston Herald after the war, I had exceptional opportunities to travel with note book and camera and meet interesting people, from old ladies who lived in haunted houses with forty cats, to President Calvin Coolidge," he wrote in his foreword to the 1955 book edition of "More Yankee Yarns." "I covered fires, floods, shipwrecks and celebrities, always watching for the unusual, human interest angle. I poked through country cemeteries and visited local libraries and historical societies."

Blackington got into the radio business in 1933, and, for the next 20 years, "Yankee Yarns" was a fixture on WBZ, being syndicated throughout New England on the NBC network.

With this background, it wasn't surprising that Blackington should find suitable material in the legend of the Old Rindge House. It wasn't until 1956, however, that he published his own account of the legend, in the June edition of Yankee magazine, entitled "The Rindge House Mystery." It appears that the house had been demolished by this point, as Blackington states, "I shall always regret that I did not go to Rindge when I first heard this story, but like a great many other things, I put it off until too late. I delayed until after the house had been torn down, but I did find some of the timbers, the cellar walls, and an old well partially filled with water."

What followed was a fanciful

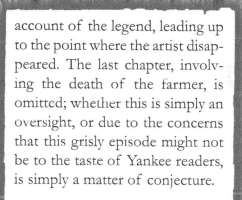

account of the legend, leading up to the point where the artist disappeared. The last chapter, involving the death of the farmer, is omitted; whether this is simply an oversight, or due to the concerns that this grisly episode might not be to the taste of Yankee readers, is simply a matter of conjecture.

Afterww

hat I hope to have accomplished in this volume is a sense of continuance -- a realization that history isn't just a series of names and dates in dusty old books, but the lives of real people, with their own worries, their own joys and sorrows, their own concerns about the world in which they lived.

In the course of this narrative, I have attempted to paint as clear a picture of early 19th century West Rindge as I can. Richard Kimball, for instance, was a minister during the period described. He also had a thriving concern in the manufacturing of clothespins.

Are there such things as ghosts, and was the Old Rindge House visited by the supernatural? Really, I have no idea; all I know is, like the Fat Boy in Dickens' "Pickwick Papers," I have a humble goal: "I wants to make your flesh creep."

Eric Stanway
December 15, 2011

Photomontage by the author

This is a photomontage with Dwight Shepler's drawing, showing the Old Rindge House, superimposed over the site, as it looks today.

Made in the USA
Charleston, SC
10 March 2012